DR. SINGH'S SCHOOL OF CHILDREN

MINDSET IS A SUPERPOWER!

THE SUPERPOWER OF CREATIVITY

DR. SINGH'S SCHOOL OF CHILDREN

MINDSET IS A SUPERPOWER!

THE SUPERPOWER OF CREATIVITY

BINAY SINGH

HTTPS://TWAGAA.COM

HTTPS://TWAGAA.COM

Mumbai (MH), India
Website: https://twagaa.com
Email: hello@twagaa.com

First published by TWAGAA INTERNATIONAL 2020

Title: Dr. Singh's School of Children : Mindset is a Superpower : The Superpower of Creativity

ISBN: 978-93-91254-84-1

First Edition
Printed in India

Ordering Information:
Quantity sales: Special discounts are available on quantity purchases by corporations, associations, and others. For details, contact the publisher at the address or email above.

ACKNOWLEDGEMENTS

I am so blessed by our great Almighty that he gave me such a blessing that I always love to be with our children. I visited an orphanage - “Ribnikov’s Children Orphanage”- with my bosom friend Misha, my recent good friend Anton Korynevych- Representative of Ukrainian president for Crimean region - and one of my best friends, Timur Korotkiy.

After meeting eight cute boys and a beautiful girl, I was very inspired to write a book for their positivity and bright careers. I believe that if I write books on Children’s Soft Skills, these books will be very helpful for children across the globe.

I am very grateful to my mother for her kind blessing to write this book series, “Dr. Singh’s School of Children”. And I am very thankful to my family and my son for their kind support to write this book series.

I am more than grateful to my friend Timur Korotkiy for his awesome and inspiring Foreword.

Acknowledgements

My sincere thanks to my friend Amy for her kind help in structuring this book properly.

Thanks to everyone in this world for their kind blessing and support.

CONTENTS

1 Introduction 9

2 How to Foster Your Child's Creativity 13

3 Help Your Little One Become Creative 19

4 Be a Superhero or I'll Switch Off the WIFI 25

5 Fun Activities and Exercises to Teach Imagination 33

6 How to Help Build a Child's Imagination 45

7 Conclusion 53

About the Author 55

More Books By Dr Binay Singh 57

INTRODUCTION

Every parent wants their kid to follow the rules - behave in school and listen to their teachers. However, there's a time and place for that. Being a leader means understanding the rules and knowing when to break or question them. It means knowing when to stand up to a teacher and how to do it right. Leaders are not born; they're made through the development of leadership skills.

Now, if your kid wants to become a leader, he needs to be creative.

This book is all about the amazing tips on developing self-esteem, creativity and leadership qualities in your child.

TEACH YOUR CHILDREN TO ASK QUESTIONS AND FIND SOLUTIONS TO PROBLEMS

As a parent it can be hard to control the urge to give a simple answer to your children's homework questions. They can get stuck on the wording or which of the answers is right because of how the teacher taught them to answer it. It's better to have them question everything about it. Question the instructions, not just on what it means but also what else it could mean if it weren't worded the same. "Find the biggest number," can mean the number with the largest value. However, it can also mean the one that's physically printed the largest!

By working with them to ask the right questions and find solutions on their own, you give them the tools to become leaders.

Now, let's delve deeper into it.

HOW TO FOSTER YOUR CHILD'S CREATIVITY

Lots of people mistakenly believe that you're born creative - that you're either good at math and science or you're good at art and music. This is not true at all. Creativity can be fostered and learned the same as any other subject or topic.

 BUY AND HAVE OPEN-ENDED TOYS

What is an open-ended toy? It's not a plastic sandal. It's anything that can be used to build something from a child's imagination into reality. The classic example is Lego. While Lego sets come with instructions and an object ready, a bucket of miscellaneous Legos can cause a child's creativity to flourish! The Lego movie captures this idea perfectly. Let them build the upside downtown of their dreams with two ice cream stores. Other good options are building blocks for more houses of their own making, and clothing to play dress up with their siblings and be their own new superheroes!

 REDUCE SCREEN TIME

Smartphones and tablets have added so many great distractions for your kid. It's made dinner time, travel time and your workdays during quarantine much easier. It's even given them a fun educational outlet! But it also has taken away from your child's creativity by displaying images and making decisions for them. How do you reduce the amount of time they spend playing with the object they love best and use most?

The easiest solution is to schedule it and do it with them. Have everyone in the family place their phones and tablets in a bag, and turn off the TV. The first couple of times will be hard but eventually it'll be a daily scheduled event and they'll forget it wasn't always around. An easy way to help get them excited about this time block is to start it with a snack. While it might feel a little weird to treat your kid like a dog, Pavlov knew what he was talking about!

ENCOURAGE IMAGINATIVE PLAY

Creativity and imagination go hand-in-hand like the peanut butter and jelly you put on their sandwiches every morning. Imaginative play is exactly what it sounds like. How can you encourage it? By giving them a good environment and multiple other children to play with. To create a good environment, all you have to do is provide the tools for them to create.

In an outdoor setting there are a lot of options. One option is chalk for hopscotch and any other games they make up. Another is plastic swords for pirates versus ninjas versus samurai versus knights!

Indoors you can provide clothing and accessories for them to come up with their own Disney princesses, princes, and characters. You can also have arts and craft supplies ready-to-go such as multi-colored construction paper, safety scissors, glue, crayons, and colored pencils.

ASK QUESTIONS ABOUT THEIR CREATIONS

While spending hours and hours on arts and crafts is great for expressing creativity, it can empty out their build up of imagination. One of the easiest ways to keep children excited and give them ideas for their next project is by asking them questions. Not just about what they made and their decisions with it, but also about the process as well. Once you figure out what they were trying to show and how they did it, don't give them advice on how to do it better. Rather encourage them to keep going and keep trying!

BE CREATIVE WITH THEM

Creating arts and crafts with your child comes with many benefits. Aside from being a great bonding activity, having your kid see you be creative inspires them to keep going when they start to get bored or run out of ideas. You can also inspire and energize them by participating with them. While working with safety scissors might make you feel too cautious, it can also be great fun!

 **CHANGE YOUR ENVIRONMENT**

While everyone has been trapped inside as of late, changing your surroundings can do wonders for your child's curiosity and creative juices. It doesn't have to be in a new house or out to a store. Spending some time in the backyard, or an empty park can accomplish this. Bring along some arts and crafts for a new place for your little Picasso to spread their wings!

 **ENCOURAGE POSSIBILITIES IN THOUGHT**

Every parent wishes they had Professor X's mind reading abilities. Unfortunately, none of us were born with that kind of luck. The best way to foster possibilities in your child's mind is by keeping a questioning attitude. Ask them 'what if' or 'what about' in as many different ways as possible. It's a little payback for all the 'why's' you get from them, but in a constructive way! Ask these questions about their imaginary characters, their artwork, and their day-to-day activities. The goal is to get them away from what things are meant to do and start thinking about what they can do with it or use it for!

 **KEEP YOUR TOYS SIMPLE**

Staying away from battery not included and completely plastic toys are two good rules of thumb. Not every toy needs to be open ended, but it's much better to have their toys able to interact without a remote, that can be used to control the main toy and will not require any creativity or imagination.

☛ HAVE IDEA AND BRAINSTORMING SESSIONS

Sometimes all your child really needs to practice their creativity is a spark from you. While they already have a foundation of imagination, they can get lost on what to start next. An easy way to do this is by having conversations about their imaginary worlds. Ask how their imaginary friend is doing. What kind of place do all their Legos live in? Do they eat other Legos or real food? By asking questions that your child hasn't thought of yet, you'll stir their creativity in coming up with answers. This will also help them build their imaginary world.

There are many different activities and practices that can help build and express your child's creativity. The most important thing is to start trying out different approaches and going with the one that sticks like their Elmer's glue!

HELP YOUR LITTLE ONE BECOME CREATIVE

 EMBRACE FAILURE

Good grades are important, as is succeeding in other activities. But you kid is human and won't succeed at everything they try. Learning how to fail in a healthy manner is important. Learning from their mistakes and understanding why they failed is more important than if they just got it right in the first place. They need to understand that it's ok to fail as long as they get up and try again, with what they learned helping them the second, third and fourth times.

 PRACTICE NEGOTIATING WITH THEM

We're not talking about letting them take hostages and play 'Die Hard'. Practice negotiating when it comes to chores, brushing their teeth, making their bed, and everything else they don't want to do. By working with them and rewarding them, you teach them value. While you might not be willing to give them a piece of chocolate, 15 more minutes of reading a book or playing a video game could be worth them making their bed right now.

 ENCOURAGE WORK AND OPPORTUNITIES

Many times, parents will say it takes too much to set up a real lemonade stand. However, giving your child the opportunity to run a 'small business' or have real-world experience in a safe place is a huge learning opportunity. Having them in charge gives them confidence and experience, which are very necessary to become a future leader in the business and non-business world.

Similarly, summer camps are a great opportunity for your child. Many summer camps build in lots of group activities that force everyone in the group to be a leader. Whether it's picking which trail they head down on a hike, or what animal costume they build, or what color represents their cabin.

PLAY GAMES TOGETHER

Family game nights can be a great way to instill some leadership skills if done right. Aside from being a great way for the family to spend some quality time together, it provides a safe space for your child to make decisions and face the consequences on their own. It gives them a chance to think strategically and come up with ways to win with certain rules in place. Win or lose, it also teaches them to be a good sport.

JOIN A SPORTS TEAM

There's a reason soccer, little league, pee wee football and others are so popular. Getting physical exercise in and tiring out your child is important. What's even more important is the learning experience that comes from it. By working together, it gives your kid a chance to ask questions on how to improve and to learn from others. Eventually they will get the chance to teach others on their team or play a leadership role, simply by encouraging the other members of their team.

BOOST THEIR CREATIVITY

There are many ways to improve your kid's creativity and imagination. One of the most important traits a leader can have is finding unique solutions to new problems. This can be a little difficult for a child to do but can be built up. The first step is to have them stop looking at things and asking, 'What is this meant to do?', and start asking 'What can I do with this?' By thinking about the world in what it can be, they can start to build solutions to problems they face and become true leaders, just like Tony Stark!

VOLUNTEER TOGETHER

Working together in groups in the real world is a great experience for your child to have. Even better is that in groups of volunteers, there's always an organizer or a leader! Volunteering together will give your child great examples of real-world leaders they can interact with and learn from. It's also never too early to start on that college application resume!

MORE READING TIME

There are lots of benefits to having your child read more. Exposure to new imaginary worlds and subjects fosters intellectual growth and progress. It gives them new perspectives on the world and opens their mind to new possibilities. These are all traits and skills a leader will need.

LET THEM PAVE THEIR OWN WAY

Making decisions from a long list of choices is an important task that all leaders must do. By letting your child make their own choices early in a safe environment, you'll help them practice leadership in action. Even something as simple as which sports team to play on or which book to read will give them self-confidence in their decisions and experience making them. They'll learn that they can't pick everything they want at one time, that there's give and take in every decision they make.

Creating the next President of the United State of America or CEO of a fortune 500 company isn't easy. With these activities you can be safely on your way to developing a great leader!

Do you love reading stories?
Let me tell you a story!

BE A SUPERHERO
OR I'LL SWITCH OFF THE WIFI

The lockdown has been quite a shocker for us. Having to spend 24 hours, 7 days a week coexisting with our children has forced us to reconnect with the reality of things outside the technology we became so dependent on.

Not only did it bring back memories but it also reminded us of how important actual playing is. This playtime is so important for their development, and because we are constantly changing our priorities, children are being left behind.

Karma works in mysterious ways... We hadn't realised how much the current situation was going to push us to reconsider those priorities and wake us up from our daily routine trance to show how our children really are important.

The fact of the matter is that we are limiting our children's capabilities by handing them technology to babysit them so that we can... watch Netflix? Be on Facebook?

Since the lockdown started, because we've been home-schooling (like most people, pretty much) we've finally seen the light. We've been given the chance to naturally assess our children's development and to realise how much we've been missing and how much impact that may be having on their development.

Going back to school has also been a traumatizing experience (for the lack of a better word), I had no idea how much I'd forgotten over the years, which makes me doubt the use of school's curriculums...And it has been painfully embarrassing.

However, all this experience has given me the chance to reconnect with the human side of my children, the non-avatar side, their non-pixeled side. I already know it's refreshing for us all.

So, I brought some old games back into our lives. Back for me. For them, it's all relatively new and even somewhat exciting, even though there are no game controllers and no levels to achieve.

So, let's take a look at how useful can they be? Walk with me here.

- Musical Chairs: Competing for a place
- What Time is it Mr Wolf: Respecting authority
- Pass The Parcel: Patience
- Hopscotch: Teamwork

- Skipping: Focus, concentration, teamwork
- Tag: Problem skipping
- Hide & Seek: Strategic planning
- Chinese Whispers: - Ensure clear message, avoid misunderstandings
- Hangman: Strategic thinking, logic, taking risks
- Doctors & Vets, Families, Shops, Cooking & Superheroes: Role-playing

The role-playing is probably one of the most enjoyable ones for them, and most valuable. Children love pretending to be adults (And I confess, I loved pretending to be one too… Lol!)

They would bring all their soft toys together down to the living room and line them up on the sofa like they were patients waiting to be called in for their appointment. Sometimes I played the Doctor, other times they did. And we would give out prescriptions (or better "perskitions") and ask them to rebook another appointment for review.

Then my daughter (11) would pretend to be the mom while my son (9) would be the mischievous child, always getting told off and shown how to behave. People management skills right here!

Sometimes we play families and we swap places. My daughter becomes me and my son the dad. It's a good opportunity to actually find out what I'm doing wrong and what other more friendly approaches to their development I can introduce. I found out that my three most popular sentences are: "Please be quiet", "No dinner, no dessert" and "If you don't do it, I will switch off the WIFI".

Playing shops has made them apply their maths skills, working out their change and about spending. These financial skills are priceless. You'll probably say: "But they can learn about these when collecting and trading coins and other 'valuable' items in video games". Maybe, but that won't teach them how to save money and how to budget for a REAL valuable item.

Cooking is not only a life-skill but it can prove to be very useful on a day when you have no plans for dinner. All children love to put their hands on dough, but this one you can actually cook. So, make pizza night a fun learning event. But make sure they clean up afterwards, otherwise it will only count as half a lesson.

The new batch of superheroes and rise of boxsets has led to a new hope for the imagination and "beyond". Children are becoming followers of this resurgent trend, where they get the chance of dressing up alongside adults, without feeling awkward.

The difference is their input for inspiration is again coming from our old TV set, rather than comic books, but the imagination is now being taken to a new level with the whole new CGI (Computer-generated Imagery) experience, which as the name suggests, allows not-real scenes to look more real and also allows real scenes to be smoother and more action-packed. You are more likely now, than ever before, to see a racoon carrying a space gun.

Once you throw the VR into the mix, they are now in an environment with full on role-play, designed by the big movies and games creators and producers. They can be THE superhero IN the movie.

Playing with a grownup opens a window to the reality that they don't normally have contact with and don't see on TV. These life-skills exercises have opened a new perspective for them, one they should already have grasped. I did, when I was their age, and that's what makes me believe that everything happens for a reason, this pandemic had an underlying reason, with its negative side too, sadly.

The pandemic has pulled families together in a time where the trend was increasingly playing with a thousand faceless players but apart. My hope is that even when we get back to normal, we can continue this rejuvenated play of old.

FUN ACTIVITIES AND EXERCISES TO TEACH IMAGINATION TO CHILDREN

Imagination is the part of our brain that makes magic happen. It allows us to adventure in far off places, be our heroes for a brief time, or simply turn a boring toilet paper roll into a peg-legged pirate's spyglass. It's something everyone should have, but it doesn't always come naturally. So, today we're going to outline fun kids' activities that develop the power of imagination. Once kids develop an imagination, the doctor's office waiting room, boring car rides, or days in the park become so much more. They become exciting adventures, and they definitely beat sitting around being bored or bouncing off the walls because there's nothing else to do.

THE GEOGRAPHY GAME

This is a fun one that's a bit educational, too. However, it's mostly for slightly older kids. 8-year olds and up should have no problem playing this one.

It's super easy. Just pick one person to start, and they can pick any real-life place they want. For example the first person can say, "China". The next person has to think of another place that begins with the last letter of the place the first player mentioned. So, if the first person said "China", Argentina, Alabama, and any other place that starts with the letter "A" will work.

This keeps going, and whenever a player takes too long to think of a real place, they're out of the game. The last person in the game is the winner!

This is a great game for long road trips, because kids can see all kinds of new places to use in the game!

 THE ANIMAL GAME

This is another super easy, completely free, game that makes boring periods a lot more fun. To start it off, the parent has to think of an animal. It can be any animal, but try to find something a little silly to keep things interesting.

Once the parent picks an animal, they have to say "I'm thinking of an animal..." and give one clue about what it is. If it's a pig, a great one would be, "and it has a curly tail". The kids then take turns guessing what the animal is, and every time they're wrong, the parent has to give another clue.

Once someone picks the right animal, they get to think of an animal and start giving out clues.

This game can be played just about anywhere, and it's a lot of fun for kids of all ages!

GROUP STORYTELLING

For this activity, it's time to tell some stories. Except, unlike reading a book, everyone gets to jump in on the fun!

This activity makes kids use their imagination, and it allows them to come up with anything they want.

To start off, start telling a story. It can be about anything, but keep it fun and lighthearted. Here's a story prompt to get you started:

"One day, Jimmy was enjoying a long walk through the woods. He saw flowers, trees, squirrels, and even pretty deer. Eventually, Jimmy came across a giant ditch with a mossy log laying across it like a bridge. He started to walk across it carefully, but then...".

Once "but then" or "and then" is said, one of the kids gets to add to the story. They can come up with anything they want, but they have to end it with "and then" so someone else gets to take a turn adding to the story. By the end of it, the group has come up with its very own story!

This one requires a bit more time than the other games, but it's really fun for car rides, waiting at the doctor's office, or slow, rainy days in the house.

CAR BINGO

Car bingo is a really fun game for kids older than 6 years, and it's perfect for long trips when they'll see a lot of new and exciting things. However it takes a bit of computer know-how.

Using Paint, or another picture editing app, add 12 pictures to a printer-paper sized image like a bingo board. You can also find ready-to-go car bingo boards all over the internet that you can just print out.

As everyone's traveling, the kids look for the items in the pictures, and they cross them off when they see them. The first person to complete a row yells out "Bingo!".

As an added bonus, keep candy or another treat up front to give to the winner. This will help with those short-attention spans that kids are known for, since they'll know they have a goodie to earn.

THE LICENSE-PLATE GAME

This game has been around forever, and it's a good game during vacations when kids get bored riding in the car for so long. It's really simple, too. Everybody plays at once.

To play, just look at the license plates of cars driving by. Each time someone sees a new state, they call it out. It helps to have a piece of paper and a pen to keep track of each state you see. The goal is to find every state before finally getting where you're headed.

TWO TRUTHS AND A LIE

This is a fun game that actually encourages kids to lie a bit. That's a welcome break from getting scolded for it all the time!

To start off, tell the kids to come up with two truths and one lie about what they did at school, or anything else. The kids then tell you all three, and you have to figure out which one is the lie.

Not only is this a fun game that makes the kids put on their thinking caps to come up with a good lie, but it also helps you bond with your kids and learn a little bit about how their day went.

TEACH THE PARENTS

This activity puts the kids in charge. Instead of the parent always teaching the kids stuff, the kids get to quiz their parents a little.

To start off, the kids have to think about what they learned at school that day, and then ask their parents to answer the same questions they had to. If the parents get it right, they get a point, if not, the kid gets bragging points for being smarter than their parents!

This not only helps kids be imaginative by pretending to be a teacher for a bit, but it also helps them comprehend their school work better as they have to remember what they were taught in order to ask the questions.

MAD, SAD, AND GLAD

This is the perfect family activity for a dinner time chat, and it can get pretty silly if you encourage acting out what happened.

It's also really simple. Everyone just takes turns talking about one thing that made them mad, one thing that made them sad, and one thing that made them glad during that particular day. Kids have to really think about their day to get one situation for each feeling, and it's a great way for the family to bond.

To make it extra-fun, encourage the kids to dramatically act out what happened. Not only do they get to be silly for a bit, but you get a bit of dinner time theater to laugh at and enjoy, without turning on the tv or whipping out your phone.

ICE BREAKERS

Every family likes to talk at the dinner table, but it's not always easy to get started. This game makes it easy to start a conversation, and it encourages everyone to have fun!

It takes a little prep, though. Mom and dad should write down questions that make the kids think creatively on index cards. Here are a few ideas:

"If you could have any super power, what would it be?"
"If you got to build any playhouse you could dream of, what would you add to it?"
"If you were the president of your class, what rules would you make?"

These are fun questions that encourage kids to think outside the box, and they let their imaginations run wild.

Once you have all your index cards made, pass them around

the dinner table and have everyone take turns answering the questions on their cards.

Encourage answers that are bonkers or not really possible. If the kids want to turn their playhouse into a rocket ship with a giant toaster on the roof, that's perfectly fine. It's all about being imaginative.

 SPOT THE MISTAKE

This one lets the kids get a bit silly, and it makes them chip in with meal time prep. Just ask them to set the table, but tell them to do something wrong on purpose. Then, you come in and find what they did wrong. They shouldn't do anything too off the wall like hiding all the plates under the sink, but things like flipping a fork upside down, putting the spoons on top of the drinking glasses, or other silly things are perfect.

 WHAT'S IN THE BAG?

What's in the Bag? Is a weird sensory game kids love, and it sets their imaginations on fire. To do it, just toss weird stuff in brown paper bags. These items can be anything that feels weird.

Good things to use are slime toys, canned spaghetti and

meatballs for a messy bit of fun, cotton balls, sand, wool, and stuff like that.

Once all the bags have something weird in them, the kids take turns reaching in, without looking, and guessing what's in the bag.

The person to get the most guesses right wins the game.

This game is best for parties. It's a great excuse to get messy, and the kids can all enjoy laughing together and have more fun guessing together, instead of just having one kid do it on their own.

 THE GREAT FACE RACE

This game is another party-based game that lets you sit back and watch as the kids not only have fun, but also use a bit of that energy up and take a nap when it's all done.

For this one, you can do it two different ways:
If you're indoors, use two poster boards and crayons. Stick the poster boards next to each other on a wall in your largest, most open room.

If you're outdoors, this is the perfect time to bust out some sidewalk chalk and let them draw on the outside of your house. Don't worry. It comes right off with a spray of the hose or a little rain.

Now, separate all the kids into two teams, and line them up in the order they'll be racing in. The first person in line for each team is given a crayon or stick of sidewalk chalk, and you countdown from three.

When you say "Go!" the first two kids have to run to the wall or poster board and draw one part of a face. So, each one can draw an eye, a mouth, or any other part. Then, they run back and pass their drawing gear to the next kid, who also runs up and draws one part.

The first team to draw a whole face wins!

Parents will be happy to know that you can pick up all the supplies you need for less than $5 at a dollar store, and it's a great way to add some cheap fun to a birthday party.

 PENNY-CUP RELAY

Want to see the kids wobble across your yard like a duck over and over again? This is the perfect way to do it, and all you need are four cups and a bunch of pennies from your change jar. If you're a bit low, take two bucks to the bank and cash them in for pennies. You'll have a solid 15-minutes of fun for 2 bucks.

To set it up, just place two cups about five-feet apart on one end of your yard, and line the kids up in two equal lines at the other end. Each team gets a cup with half the pennies in it. Start it off by having the first kid in each line tuck a penny between their knees, and they have to get it across the yard and into the cup, without dropping it or using their hands. Once they put their penny in the cup, they just run back and let the next kid go.

The first team to put all their pennies in their team's cup wins! This will wear the kids out for a nap, and it's a ton of cheap fun.

HOW TO HELP BUILD A CHILD'S IMAGINATION

When you're young, a simple blanket fort is more than what meets the eye. It's a castle built by and with your family. Soaring into the sky, their own personalized house that's larger than life.

A child's imagination is more important than what you might think at first. There are more benefits to improving your kid's imagination both while they're young and later in life.

Just like any other sport or school subject, practice is what pays off the most in the long run. You'll want to keep them active in their world of pretend as much as possible in the most productive ways.

Here's some ways to help build your little one's big imagination!

 CREATE A DAILY GAME

There's lots of fun and simple games you can play with your child. You can play "spy" and need to find some secret information. Like, are the tomatoes growing outside red yet or still green? Of course, this information is needed to save the day! Detective is another great one. Solve the mystery of 'is your sibling hungry'? Do they want or need a snack? Make sure they didn't have one already! Collect any evidence you find (aka food wrappers). You can even give them a Ziplock bag and a Sharpe to number it. Just don't let them go too far with that Sharpe or your walls might pay the price!

MAKE TIME DURING OTHER ACTIVITIES

Once you've started creating simple daily games, you can make them work around your and your kid's busy schedules. Bored during the drive to and from school? Incorporate a verbal game you can play together! It could be riddle solving, a long running alphabet game (finding an object for each letter of the alphabet while driving), or the color game (same as the alphabet but for each color).

Another way to work this into your daily routine is to have your kid guess the weather and work on building what they should wear for the day. This is hard for some kids, especially ones that have a favorite superhero shirt they want to just wear every day.

SCREEN-FREE TIME

It's easy for both you and your child to get caught up in the virtual world of apps, tv shows, movies, and texting. The downside is this takes away some of the power of your kid's imagination, just because they're not using it. It's being provided to them in the form of their games on the phone or iPad. You shouldn't take it away from them entirely, as it is important for them to be immersed in technology and understand it.

The easiest way to do this is to do it with them. Schedule some screen-free time together and have everyone place their devices in a basket or box for an hour.

 GIVE THEM A FOUNDATION

While you want them to build imaginary worlds on their own, it can be hard to have a physical starting point. Once the screen is off, they'll need tools to express their imagination and creativity physically.

A great way to accomplish this is to create indoor and outdoor activity boxes. An indoor box should contain arts & crafts supplies, such as construction paper, safety scissors, glue, crayons, and pipe cleaners. You can also include clothing and plastic accessories for dress up or action adventure! An outdoor box should include washaway chalk, balls (large and small), and soft frisbees (hard if the children are older). If it's summertime, you can even include super soakers and water balloons as a great way to stay cool and active. Make sure they're not always available though, you don't want to become an aqua-parent!

LET THEM TAKE CONTROL

Your child will need you for their start into the unseen world. But make sure they know who the captain is. It's not you. You rule everything else and run their lives. In the world of imagination, they reign supreme just like King Arthur. By having them lead, you allow their imagination and creativity to expand. Their decisions and their choices matter most of all in a world of pure imagination.

CREATE ART WITH THEM

From watercolors, to macaroni cards. There are so many art projects out there that you can do with your child. If you have the time and money, a class in pottery can be a great bonding activity that will stimulate their imagination and creativity. Drawing and painting are the two easiest activities that you can do with them. The easiest way to inspire them on what to draw or paint is to pick a topic ahead of time (but only if your child isn't ready to take the lead with their own idea!)

TELL THEM STORIES AND LET THEM BE INVOLVED

Children love tall tales and stories of their parents and relatives from when they were younger (whether they're exaggerated or not). Telling them stories stirs their creativity and helps build their imagination in the many directions a story can go. In order to get them to really expand it, they also have to practice. A great way to do this is to build a story with them involved! Have everyone in the family sit around the table and start the story yourself, have the next person add the next step, and so on. This kind of collaboration will most likely be very goofy, involve silly actions and statements. That's great! Remember your role here is to have their input valued by going with the flow.

EMBRACING BOREDOM

While all these activities and practices are necessary and great, there's one thing above all else that will help your child build their imagination, forcing them to embrace it. And that's simply being bored. With all the forms of stimulus that exist in our technology driven world of smart phones, smart tvs and tablets, there are few pure brain breaks. Once your kid has some time alone with just their thoughts, they'll be able to build up their creative juices and imagination for the next practice activity. It's a bit like a superhero recovering after each of their fights. They can't face Ultron every day without a break!

There are many ways to give your child's imagination practice. Just ensure to keep them at it!

CONCLUSION

All modern day and historical inventions were a result of someone's curiosity about how the world around them worked. From the very first toilet, the printing press for books, to Edison's lightbulb, to computers, and of course the internet! Make sure your children know the most important part is to question everything. Why do we do this a certain way? How can I solve this problem? How can I get out of cleaning my room?

While sometimes getting barraged, like a war veteran, with questions can be annoying, answering them in the right way will grow your child's creativity enough for them to benefit from it. After all, who doesn't want their child to be a great inventor.

ABOUT THE AUTHOR

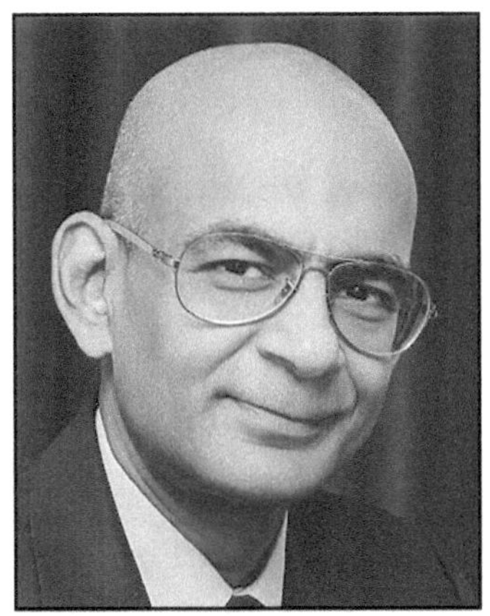

Dr Binay Kumar Singh, Founder & CEO of *Singh Marine Management Ltd.* in Odessa (Ukraine) and Founder & President of *Federation of Global Maritime Community*, is an entrepreneur, author, and public speaker. His life mission is to serve the world's communities and guide everyone through positivity, love, and enthusiasm. This is reflected in his simple and timeless life philosophy: "Treat people as you like to be treated."

Dr Singh has a Master of Science in Marine Navigation and a Doctorate of Philosophy. He is a globally recognized expert in international shipping with over two decades of experience. Dr Singh is also taking wonderful measures for the needy community of the society as well. His new project with the name "Selfless Fund" is specifically targeted to help those who are in need. Dr Singh has also launched his new company GSR which is going to bring innovations to the shipping and maritime industry. His efforts for the shipping industry as well as for the society is an example of his generosity and selflessness.

He enjoys pursuing multiple passions like singing, dancing, playing the piano and the accordion, and keeping healthy by practicing yoga and CrossFit.

Email: binaysingh@gsr.international
Website: https://drbinaysingh.com

MORE BOOKS BY DR BINAY SINGH

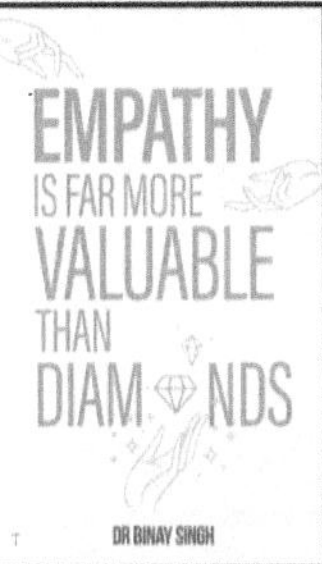

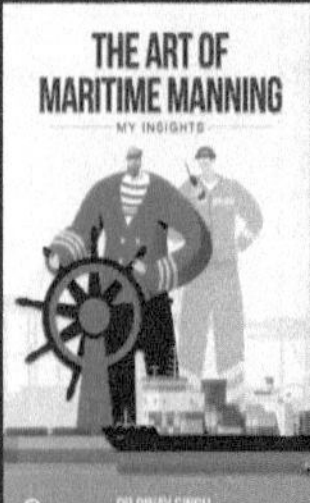
THE ART OF
MARITIME MANNING
MY INSIGHTS
DR BINAY SINGH

THE
ART
NEGOTIATION
DR SINGH'S INSIGHTS
DR BINAY SINGH

THE
ART
SMARTPHONE-LIFE BALANCE
DR SINGH'S INSIGHTS
DR BINAY SINGH

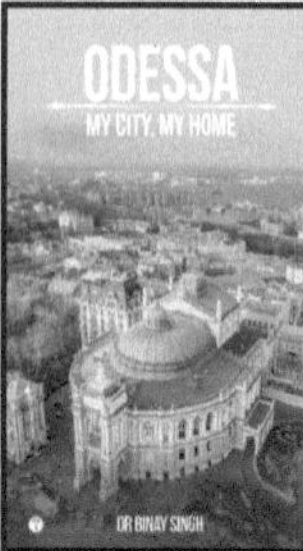
ODESSA
MY CITY, MY HOME
DR BINAY SINGH

DIGITAL ADDICTION
KEEP YOURSELF AND YOUR FAMILY SAFE
DR BINAY SINGH

THE
ART
OF
TEAM MANAGEMENT
DR SINGH'S INSIGHTS
DR BINAY SINGH

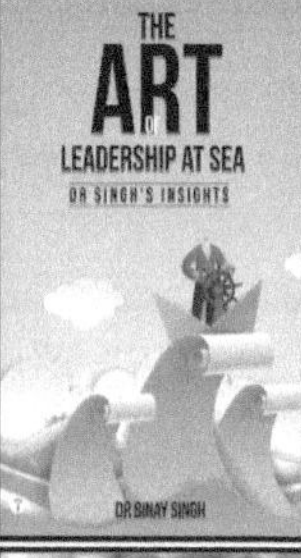
THE
ART
LEADERSHIP AT SEA
DR SINGH'S INSIGHTS
DR BINAY SINGH

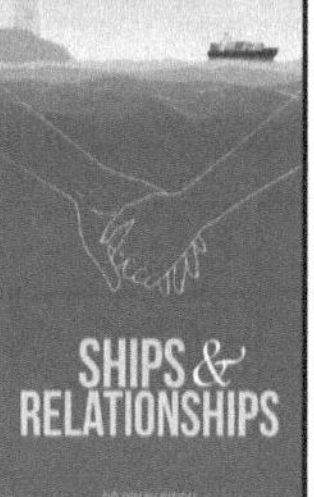
SHIPS &
RELATIONSHIPS
DR BINAY SINGH

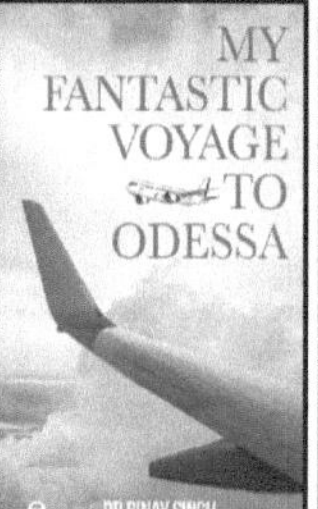
MY
FANTASTIC
VOYAGE
TO
ODESSA
DR BINAY SINGH

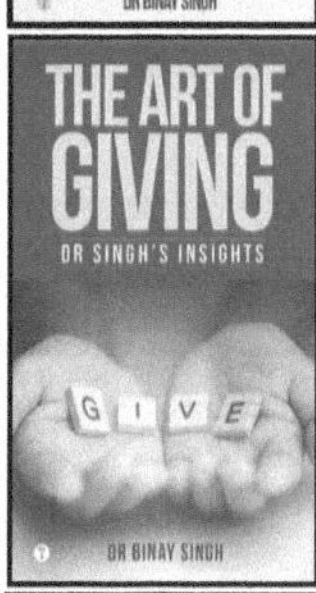
THE ART OF
GIVING
DR SINGH'S INSIGHTS
GIVE
DR BINAY SINGH

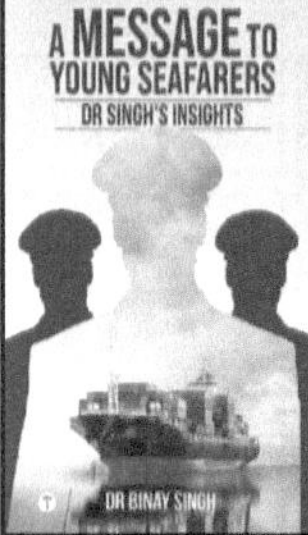
A MESSAGE TO
YOUNG SEAFARERS
DR SINGH'S INSIGHTS
DR BINAY SINGH

Svetlana
DR BINAY SINGH

THE
ART
OF
MOTIVATIONAL
SPEAKING
DR SINGH'S INSIGHTS
DR BINAY SINGH

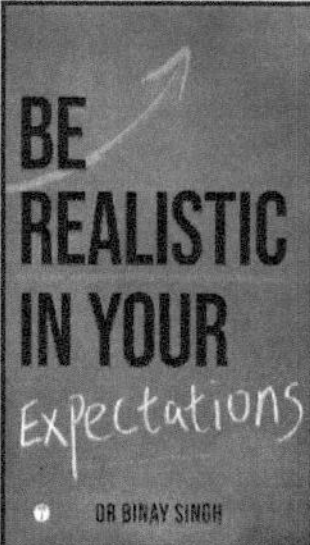
BE
REALISTIC
IN YOUR
Expectations
DR BINAY SINGH

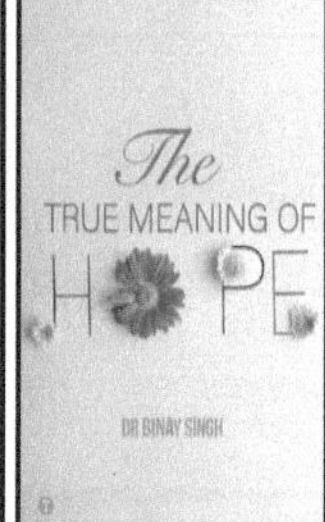
The
TRUE MEANING OF
HOPE
DR BINAY SINGH

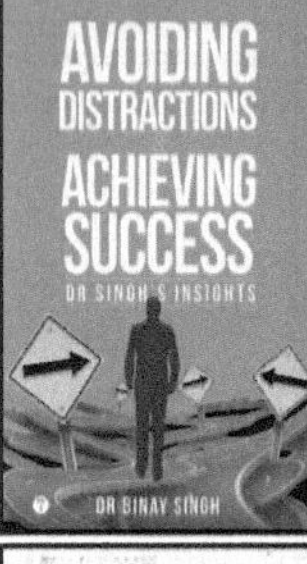
AVOIDING
DISTRACTIONS
ACHIEVING
SUCCESS
DR SINGH'S INSIGHTS
DR BINAY SINGH

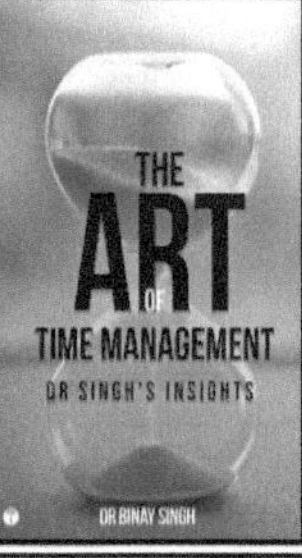
THE
ART
OF
TIME MANAGEMENT
DR SINGH'S INSIGHTS
DR BINAY SINGH

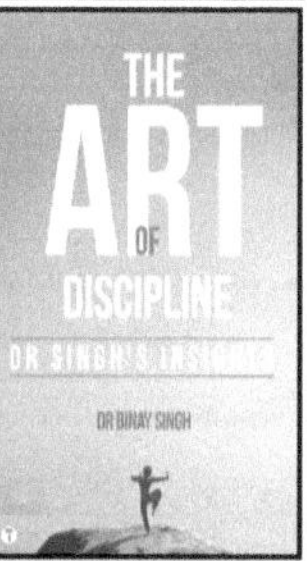
THE
ART
OF
DISCIPLINE
DR SINGH'S INSIGHTS
DR BINAY SINGH

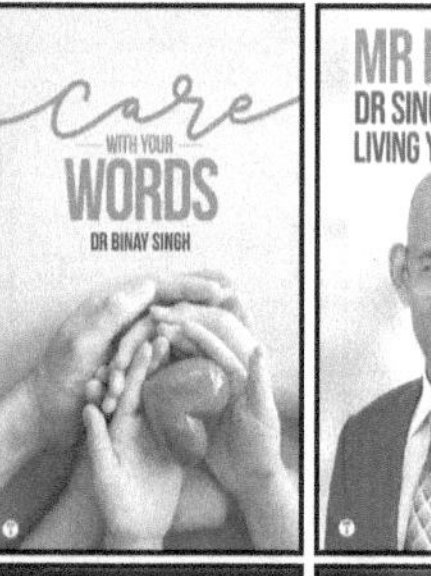
Care
WITH YOUR
WORDS
DR BINAY SINGH

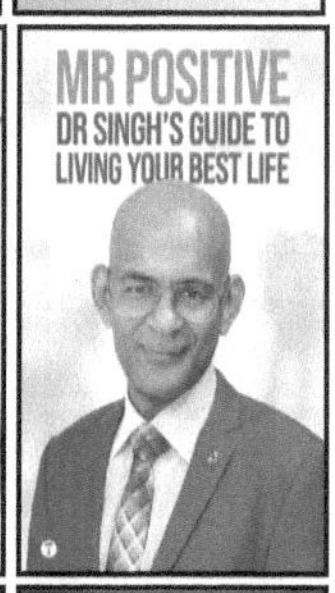
MR POSITIVE
DR SINGH'S GUIDE TO
LIVING YOUR BEST LIFE

THE
Magic
OF MUSIC
DR SINGH'S INSIGHTS
DR BINAY SINGH

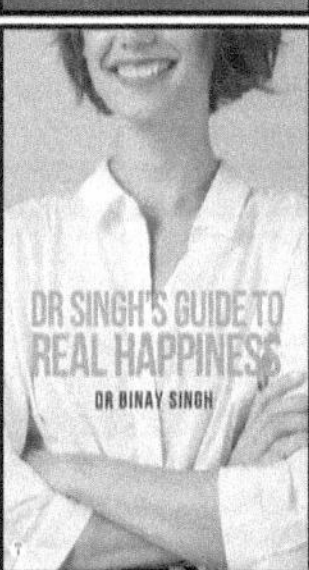
DR SINGH'S GUIDE TO
REAL HAPPINESS
DR BINAY SINGH

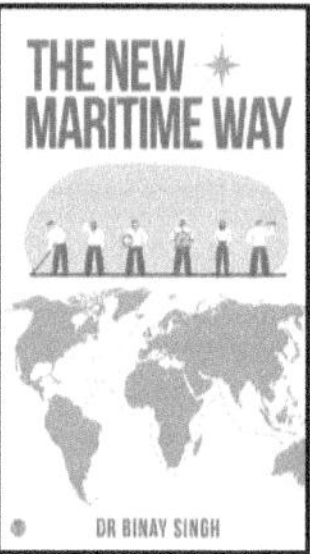
THE NEW
MARITIME WAY
DR BINAY SINGH

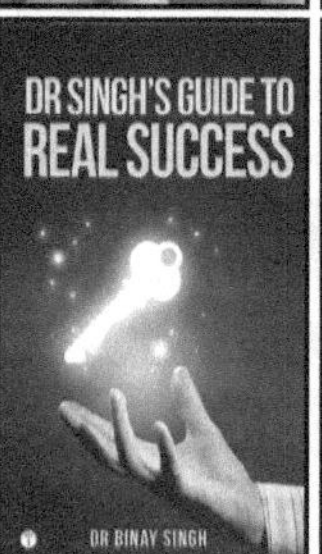
DR SINGH'S GUIDE TO
REAL SUCCESS
DR BINAY SINGH

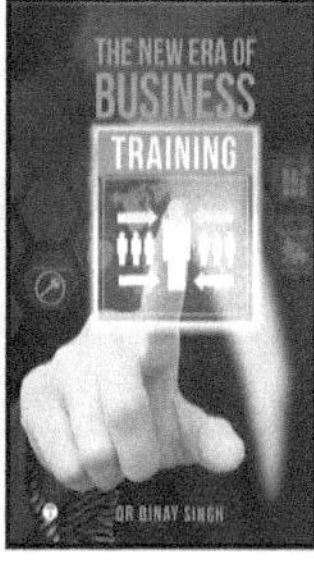
THE NEW ERA OF
BUSINESS
TRAINING
DR BINAY SINGH

www.ingramcontent.com/pod-product-compliance
Lightning Source LLC
LaVergne TN
LVHW090139160826
845673LV00017B/2524

* 9 7 8 9 3 9 1 2 5 4 8 4 1 *